TOKYO

This book was devised and produced by
Multimedia Publications (UK) Ltd

Editor: Marilyn Inglis
Production: Arnon Orbach
Design: John Strange and Associates
Picture Research: Paul Dowswell

Copyright © Multimedia Publications (UK) Ltd 1984

First published in the United States of America 1985 by
Gallery Books, an imprint of W. H. Smith Publishers Inc.,
112 Madison Avenue, New York, NY 10016

ISBN 0 8317 8787 2

Colour origination by D S Colour International Ltd, London
Printed in Italy by Sagdos
Typeset by Flowery Typesetters Ltd

TOKYO

Mitzi Bales

Contents

1
Inviting Diversity

Tokyo is a many-sided city. The ancient Kannon Temple, the oldest temple in Tokyo, stands very near a modern department store. The 17th century Zojoji Temple shares Shiba Park with the Tokyo Tower, an imposing monument to post World War II recovery. The Imperial Palace is old and traditional, set serenely in parkland behind walls and moats, but it borders on the bustling financial district of tall new office buildings. This meeting of the venerable and historic — the Oriental, with the contemporary and international — the Western, is one of Tokyo's more striking features.

The modernity of the city is not due to a philosophy of tearing down the old in favor of the new. Tokyo has been razed to the ground many times — twice in this century alone — by earthquakes, fire, volcanic eruptions and more recently, wartime air raids. Each time it has been rebuilt, almost from scratch and its multitude of skyscrapers reflects the extent of Western influence since the 1920s.

Tokyo ablaze with the lights of a modern city. In the background, Mount Fuji, grand and serene in the timeless moonlight. Both symbolize Japan to the world.

But Tokyo has not lost its unique personality. Where else is such a thing as the kōban found, the little boxlike structure sited on a corner in every neighborhood? People stop by endlessly to ask directions of its police occupants in a city where house addresses and street names are scarce. And the patient cops seem to know every person, shop, and alley in their area. Where else are the rooftops of numerous buildings converted into practice ranges to satisfy the national craze for golf? Where else would a bar be named God because the owners wanted a name that would stand out in a neighborhood packed with bars, and thought dog spelled backward would do the trick?

There is always something to do in Tokyo. It is a place where people go to department stores for diversion, even if they dislike shopping. They go because on any one day almost every department store will have a major art or craft exhibition, a demonstration of the tea ceremony, or a tie-in display with whichever festival is going on. The stores offer antiques, food departments as varied and extensive as supermarkets, roof gardens with cafés, pet shops and children's play areas. In fact, the local department store is often the focus of a family's Sunday outing. Another favorite for inexpensive entertainment are the coffee and tea shops dotted everywhere over the city. Many of these provide live jazz, pop, and rock music or recorded classical music, and people listen and linger over a cup of "hotto" (regular) or "American" (weak) coffee for hours. At New Year's and on the emperor's birthday at the end of April, the palace is partly open to the public and thousands pay a visit there. For the music lover there are regular concerts by seven symphony orchestras and, of the several concert halls, the Bunka Kaikan in Ueno Park is internationally famous for its excellent acoustics. There are parks, some with traditional gardens of exceptional beauty; boat rides to Asakusa, the oldest part of the city; museums and art galleries of all kinds; a hectic and exciting nightlife; classical theater in the form of Kabuki, Noh, and Bunraku; Tokyo Disneyland; modern musicals and plays, and movies galore. And there's pachinko, the pinball game whose clinking sound overrides even the noise of the traffic.

Right One of the towering luxury hotels that abound in Akasaka. The distinctiveness of this Tokyo district, not far from the Imperial Palace, is its many foreign restaurants and large modern hotels. It is one of the more cosmopolitan areas of the city, with a cluster of embassies and a nightlife of great variety.

Above Tall office buildings in Tokyo's commercial center. The architecture of the city began to look Western in the 1920s, but the piercing of the skyline with high risers dates only from the post-war period.

Left Open front shops in a local neighborhood. Here is the flavor of the Tokyo behind its Western facade: typical foods in typical stores that are not much more than a sheltered stall. The shopkeepers are at their jobs early in the morning, with much friendly chat to each other. They are known for the meticulous honesty and exceptional courtesy that marks all service in Japan.

The damper on the delights of Tokyo is the constant crush of people. Although it sprawls over many miles, the city is still not big enough for a population of some 11 million. Overcrowding is a fact of daily life. People live in pocket-size homes that make privacy almost impossible. Public transportation is a round-the-clock rush hour with the real rush hour being a crush beyond description. This would almost certainly cause tension and unrest anywhere else in the world but here the temper of the city is gentle. People bow courteously to one another as their ancestors did and violent crime is virtually unheard of.

Facing The Ginza at night. This is one of Tokyo's most famous shopping streets, bejewelled with some of the oldest and best department stores, elegant specialty shops, and delightful places for refreshment.

Left A fresh food counter in a department store. Food sections usually take up the whole of the store's basement, making them an equal of any supermarket.

Below A large coffee shop looking down on a busy street. Coffee and tea shops are everywhere and of every size, from a tight-squeeze two tables to ballroom proportions. Coffee is expensive, but one cup entitles the customer to linger for hours. The cakes and pastries are culinary masterpieces, as wonderful to the taste as to the eye.

Every new fad grabs a large and enthusiastic following and the pace of life can seem frantic. But people still find serenity in some of the traditional cultural arts, especially in the tea ceremony. This gracious ritual of drinking tea in a group had its origin in medieval Zen Buddhism. It is intended to express a love of beauty and a search for spiritual peace. Every gesture in the preparation and serving of the special powdered green tea has a meaning, and every utensil must meet high standards of beauty. The tea bowls are particularly important and are held thoughtfully and admiringly before being emptied. Once performed by monks only, today millions of pupils study the art of tea drinking.

The weather can add to Tokyo's appeal. September and October are pleasantly hot and bright, November is mild, and the winter cold is offset by sunny blue skies. March, April, and May are warm and green. Against this, June is rainy and the summer is very oppressive.

It is hard to imagine Tokyo's earliest years as a small and unimportant fishing village. However by the 17th century it had become the first national capital and some legacies from that period still remain. For example Tokyo's markedly individual neighborhoods date from the time that the shoguns divided

Facing, top An everyday scene near a city shrine. The woman in the foreground is wearing a gauze face mask to keep her cold germs from spreading. This is a common act of social conscience in a city of shocking overcrowding. Some people also wear the masks as protection from air pollution.

Facing, bottom Another scene of daily life in the capital city – people as far as the eye can see. This picture also shows how well groomed and prosperous looking most of them are, and how they conform to conventional standards of dress.

Left A golf practise range at Shiba Park. Golf is a national craze and membership of a golf club is a status symbol. It is not uncommon to see office rooftops turned into golf ranges, mostly for the executives of the companies within.

Below The floor of the stock exchange. In the wake of post-war recovery and good times, many ordinary people invest in stocks and bonds and the Tokyo exchange is a hive of activity. People are squeezed for space at work as everywhere else.

the city into districts as a security measure. For something like 200 years each district was stockaded and guarded to control all comings and goings, and the communities behind the barricades developed in their own ways. Today people go to particular quarters for books, for the latest fashions, for certain specialty foods. The atmosphere of Shimbashi is different from Akasaka, Roppongi from Ginza, Marunouchi from Nihonbashi, though all are studded with restaurants, shops, and public buildings.

In all, Tokyo is invitingly diverse. Political leaders and civil servants live here because it is the governmental capital of Japan. Artists and writers live here because it is the cultural capital of the nation. Stockbrokers and industrialists live here because it is the financial capital of the country. The city boasts about 100 colleges and universities, it is a major manufacturing and publishing center and a transportation hub. It offers activities for every taste and people flock from far and wide to become a part of it.

Above right The kōban, or police box, on a neighborhood street corner. Everyone aims for the kōban when they are seeking directions – and the police who staff it seem to know every person, alley, and store in their locality. Tokyo addresses do not follow an understandable pattern so it is not easy even for residents to find their way around.

Right Elevated expressways through a busy part of town. Tokyo is choked by traffic, and expressways like these are intended to relieve the almost constant jams in the streets beneath them. Instead, they become an elevated traffic jam during rush hours – and add nothing to the city's beauty.

Right The Shinkansen, or New Express Line, fastest train in the world. Known as the bullet train, the Shinkansen links Tokyo with Fukuoka 735 miles (1176 km) away, stopping at such major cities as Kyoto and Osaka. It is a smooth, comfortable ride, made as safe as possible by an automatic warning system that will stop the train during an earthquake or typhoon.

Below Motorcyclists revving up for action. Tokyo's young try to beat the traffic by riding motorcycles — and, of course, manage to add to the general bedlam.

Right An outdoor class in the tea ceremony in a Tokyo park. A special ritual of drinking tea is practiced as an art form in Japan, and millions study it as a social and cultural nicety. It is one of the occasions on which women will often dress up in the traditional kimono.

Right The tea ceremony of old. This print by Toshikata at the turn of the century shows some of the utensils and equipment laid out for the ritual. The tea ceremony was created by medieval Zen monks as a way of expressing a love of beauty and a search for spiritual peace. It was once performed in a special house entered by crawling through a low narrow door. This act, like the custom of naked group bathing, made everyone equal to each other.

Left The lake in Korakuen Park. This is the oldest traditional garden in Tokyo, dating from 1626, though the lake was a later addition. It is one of the most beautiful of the city's parks with its skilfully laid out displays of Japanese and Chinese plants, its little temple dedicated to the goddess of happiness, and its small teahouse. The huge Korakuen Games and Sports Center, in the eastern part of the park, offers skating, swimming, electronic games and other recreational facilities.

Facing Garden landscaping with that unmistakable Japanese touch. The position of the tree, stepping stones, and water lilies make a little composition within a larger one, for a Japanese garden is always laid out to create a unified scenic vista.

Left An azalea bonsai trained to resemble a coral reef. The raising of dwarf trees has been brought to a high art form in Japan and is one of its unique cultural features. It takes between eight and ten years to shape a bonsai as desired. There are frequent exhibits of dwarf plants in Tokyo and it is common to find nattily dressed businessmen spending their lunch hours in thoughtful contemplation of them.

Below The garden of the Tofukuji Temple. The use of sand instead of grass is unusual to the Western eye, but accords with the Japanese fashion established centuries ago. The five moss-covered mounds represent formerly sacred mountains.

19

Imperial Past

Asakusa, one of Tokyo's oldest districts. The foreground looks much as it would have in the seventeenth century when Tokyo was known by its old name of Edo. The background shows the sharp contrast of the modern buildings, which make it look like any other city in the world. The shoguns marked Asakusa out as the working class quarters.

Unlike most European capitals, Tokyo did not always hold that honor, nor did it evolve naturally into that position. Like Washington D.C., it was made into the capital. This was accomplished by the first Tokugawa shogun, Ieyasu, who began his rule of Japan in 1603. Leaving the figurehead emperor in the old capital of Kyoto, Ieyasu transformed the sleepy little village of Edo into his center of power, and the years of rule from here are called the Edo period.

Edo, or Yedo, was probably about 500 years old at the start of the Tokugawa rule. It was located in a wooded marshy area that had not encouraged growth, but it had been fortified by a castle in 1457 and had become the provincial capital only a few years before Ieyasu Tokugawa came upon the scene. In fact, it was on the site of Edo Castle that the Tokugawas established their

residence and lived for the next 265 years.

It was natural that the court aristocrats drew merchants to sell to them, artisans to supply their personal and household needs, artists and entertainers to satify their cultural taste, as well as officials, servants and laborers. And so Edo grew. Then in 1634 the shogunate, as a way of control, made it law that every family of every daimyo (feudal lord) had to live in Tokyo. The next year the law was extended to require every daimyo to join his hostage family for a period of residence each year. This artificial increase of the population was matched by the increase that always comes to a country's major city, and Edo mushroomed. By 1758 it was the largest city in the world, with a population of over a million. It had withstood a calamitous fire in 1657, when almost half the city was destroyed, and it had seen the last eruption of Mount Fuji in 1707, when its streets were showered with volcanic ash.

The Tokugawa palace, splendid and safe behind high walls and moats, was encircled by the homes of the daimyo families and the samurai (high military class). Outside this enchanted circle the administrative life of the city began and, a little further away, the commercial life. Today the palace is still the heart of the city and the area bordering its tall stone boundary is still the political and financial center.

The security-conscious shoguns divided Edo into various quarters, each of which was barricaded and guarded at its entry. Cut off in this way, the stockaded communities developed individual characters which can still be felt in the districts that make up modern Tokyo.

Edo was a bustling, thronging city for most of the nearly three centuries of Tokugawa rule although the world knew little about it. But the outside intruded on Japan and its capital in 1853 when a United States naval expedition forced the shogun to sign a foreign trade agreement. After that the inrush of new ideas and information shook and splintered the rigid structure of the shogunate. It fell to a relatively bloodless revolution in 1868, which restored the Emperor Meiji as head of the state and made the first steps toward a democratic system of government. This Meiji revolution was led by aristocrats, military officers, and nobles who had managed to learn much about Western politics, technology, and culture in spite of the shoguns' restrictions — a process that had speeded up as the shogunate inevitably wound down.

It was the Meiji government that changed the name of Edo to Tokyo, which means the "eastern capital". This was done for subtle political reasons and was connected with moving the emperor from his separate capital in the more westerly city of Kyoto. Within four years of rapid Westernization by the Meiji powers, Tokyo could boast of telegraph and railroad lines to Yokohama and a modern postal system.

Twice during the Meiji period, in 1855 and 1894, the capital rumbled and crumbled

Facing, top A six-panel screen of the seventeenth century, depicting the Portuguese arrival in Japan a century earlier. The first Westerners ever seen by the Japanese landed on the southernmost island of Kyushu in 1542 and soon established trade relations. They were confined to the city of Nagasaki and so had little effect on the everyday life of the mass of people.

Facing, bottom A view of one of the courtyards of the Imperial Palace. The architecture is typically Japanese – clean simple lines for a structure of wood with paper doors and windows. Built in the early seventeenth century, the palace was the home of all the Tokugawa shoguns for 265 years. It lies in an extensive parkland separated from the city beyond by walls and moats.

Left A guard at the entrance to the palace. The palace gardens are open to the public twice a year and by permission other days.

Below The Nijubashi Bridge, leading to the interior of the palace over the inner moat. Its name means "double bridge" and refers to how it looks reflected in the water.

under disastrous earthquakes. The 20th century was only about one fourth gone when catastrophe struck again: in September 1923 Tokyo was ravaged by an earthquake and raging fires. Most of the old part of the city simply disappeared. Its traditional wooden buildings, highly resistant to wind, flood, and tremor, were mere tinder in fires. At the quake's end, nearly half the capital lay wasted, and from 100000 to 150000 lives were lost. Among the worthy edifices that survived were the Asakusa Kannon temple in the old city, the Imperial hotel, designed by Frank Lloyd Wright with an "earthquake-proof" foundation, and the Mitsukoshi department store in the newer part.

The rebuilding of the devastated capital was accomplished quickly, in a record seven-and-a-half years. Now Tokyo began to look decidedly more Western than Asian, as many steel and reinforced concrete structures rose along wide avenues.

Continuously holding a place as one of the world's three largest cities, Tokyo reached a population of over two million in 1930 and over six million in 1941.

The most recent devastation in Tokyo's history came through human agents rather than Nature. On March 9, 1945, a World War II air attack dropped some 700000 bombs on the capital, leaving about 200000 people killed or missing. Again about half of Tokyo lay in ruins, although the palace and the congress building were among the landmarks left standing. The rebuilding was carried out along former lines, though tall buildings began to make an appearance by the mid-1960s. By then Tokyo had enough pride in itself to welcome and accommodate the 1964 summer Olympics. Much of the planning for these involved street widening, sanitary improvements, rapid transport expansion, and building of a kind that would enhance the city dramatically and permanently.

In 1978 the tallest building in all of Asia was constructed in Tokyo. Known as Sunshine City, it is a skyscraper of 60 stories reaching 792 ft (240 m) in height. It heralded other towering skyscrapers, which are clustered mostly in the Shinjuku district. This creates a city architecture as different from the 12th-century Edo as a computer is from an abacus. Today some 11 million people go about their daily lives in this great metropolis that has picked itself up, dusted itself off, and won the race several times in its history.

Right A suit of armor from about 1750. The artisans of the period were famous for their work with metals, not only for weaponry but also for domestic wares.

Above A modern swordmaker. Techniques of the craft have been handed down from generation to generation, and the artisans today still work in traditional informal kimono. Their products now sell as souvenirs, prized more for beauty than efficiency.

Left Old samurai swords in a museum display. The Japanese Sword Museum in Tokyo contains modern as well as ancient examples · of the finest swordmakers' craft.

25

Facing Detail from a print of 1860 showing foreign ships off Yokohama, only 18 miles (30 km) south of Tokyo. The armed ships of Commodore Perry, under the United States flag, had forced the Japanese ruler to open the country to trade in 1853, and other nations were quick to take advantage of it. The introduction of Western ideas and technology resulted in the overthrow of the shogunate in 1868 by progressive forces.

Left The main gate of Tokyo's Meiji Shrine. One of Japan's most popular monuments, it was built to honor the first emperor after the fall of the shogunate.

Below A commercial fishing fleet in Tokyo harbor. Fishing is one of the oldest trades in Japan, natural for a people who depend on the sea as their main source of food.

Above The railway station at Shimbashi. Though it is one of the older parts of Tokyo, little of Shimbashi's antiquity is in evidence today. Still, as of old, it is a favorite entertainment district, dotted with many bars and specialty restaurants.

Right The famous skyline of skyscrapers in Shinjuku. Like all of Tokyo's various sections, Shinjuku has an individual character. It is one of the few places where muggings occur and it is sometimes shunned as the hangout of toughs, but it is also one of the city's main transportation points, serving millions of subway and train commuters daily, and it has many fine hotels, stores, and restaurants.

Facing The Ginza on Sunday, when it is closed to traffic. Sunday is a big day for family outings and almost all the stores stay open, so people delight in swarming over the street and sidewalks in pursuit of pleasure. And even a stroll along the glittering Ginza can be entertaining – if crowds and din can be taken in stride.

3
Modern Metropolis

Tokyo grew by spreading along the broad Kanto plain and absorbing dozens of villages and small towns into its fabric. It was this which created the city's higgledy-piggledy layout. The maze of streets were the roads of once unrelated settlements. Now huge elevated expressways leave the labyrinth of traffic-choked streets below in an effort to relieve jams. Unfortunately they have done neither skyline nor traffic any good.

The modern megalopolis, the Tokyo Metropolitan Area or Tokyo Prefecture, covers 81 square miles (2410 sq km). For all its size, the city is bursting with people and the density of population is expressed as 1.2 rooms per household. Such cramming of many people into small spaces would probably create slums elsewhere, but in Tokyo even the shabbiest dwelling looks spick and span, often brightened up with pots of flowers and shrubs that are tenderly cared for.

Tokyo's well-defined districts have something for everyone. Is it to be a search for a pocket calculator that translates Japanese into English? Destination Akihabara, where one electronics shop after another offers myriads of products. Is it to be shopping for costly high fashions? Off to Harajuku, where the mirrored splendor of the Hanae Mori building reflects other boutiques along the avenue. Is it to be dinner of an exotic cuisine? Akasaka is the objective, where foreign restaurants and large luxury hotels abound, and where the American Embassy is located. Is it to be a book browse? Kanda it is, then. Here one street is lined with more than a hundred second-hand bookshops, helping to make this district one of the largest concentrations of booksellers in the world.

Shinjuku is like a city within a city, its busy station engulfing and disgorging more than a million rail and subway users a day. It is a bit tawdry and even risky, known for clip joints and muggings. Shibuya is also like a small town of its own, in this case comfortably middle-class with large modern apartment buildings, good department stores, and well-tended public squares.

The Ginza district boasts two of the city's most famous and glittering prizes: the shopping thoroughfare called the Ginza, and the Kabukiza Theater. The Ginza is like New York's Fifth Avenue, London's Bond Street and Paris's Rue St Honoré in one. The best-known department stores are here, along with first-class specialty shops, less sophisticated novelty shops and the snack bars, coffee shops and restaurants that revive the weary shopper. Here and there along the street, as in other shopping areas, fortune tellers set up their portable booths for the many clients who avidly or earnestly consult them. Near the north end of this lively major street is Nihonbashi, the bridge from which all distances are measured. The

Showing itself ever a leader in modern public transportation, Tokyo offers one of the world's few monorail services. The bright red, silver, and white trains run from Hamamatsucho in the southeast of the city to Haneda Airport, which is used for internal air traffic and flights to China.

Right Another view of the Ginza on Sunday. The Ginza is a district as well as a street and both have long been known for the variety and elegance of their shops. The internationally renowned Mikimoto Pearl Company has a store here (see sign in the middle of this photograph) and one of Tokyo's best-known bookshops for English literature is near the Ginza subway station.

Below A row of stores in Akihabara. This is where the shrewd Tokyo shopper goes for everything electric and electronic, both for wide choice and for bargains – but the tourist does better to visit only for fun because the products are meant for use only with 100-watt power. Akihabara is another example of how Tokyo is composed of many districts, each with a special nature of its own, though it is not clear why this section evolved into "electronics city".

original was built in 1603, and its boldly curved arch was often painted by such renowned artists as Hiroshige. It has been rebuilt several times, and the present one is easily overlooked in the deluge of traffic that swamps it.

Architecturally the Kabukiza looks somewhat like a shrine, and is indeed a shrine for the fans of Kabuki plays, one traditional theater form of Japan. The huge edifice seats about 2600 and is full of interesting eateries, bars and souvenir stalls are worth a visit for themselves.

Asakusa, across the Sumida River that intersects the city, is one of the oldest districts. Once an unhealthy marsh, it was assigned as the living quarters of the poor by the shoguns, and it is still the most working-class area with the most traditional way of life. Its biggest attraction is the Kannon temple, which miraculously survived both the 1923 earthquake and the 1945 bombing. A long street of booths selling souvenirs and religious tokens leads up to the temple, and is usually thronged with people seeking a taste of olden times. Passenger boats ply the Sumida to Asakusa almost daily and, if good fortune brings a return trip as lights begin to twinkle on, the view of Tokyo harbor and the city behind it is absolutely breathtaking.

West of the imperial palace, which is regarded as the center of the city, is found one of Tokyo's chief landmarks – the Meiji Shrine. The Inner Garden of this extensive memorial is a wonderland of thick woods, a beautiful lake, elegant traditional buildings containing royal treasure, and a majestic main torii (gate) made of ancient Hinoki tree trunks. The famous iris garden is at its best in May, when its more than 100 varieties of the flower are in full bloom. In the Outer Garden, which is of more recent date, is the impressive National Stadium built for the 1964 Olympics.

North of the palace, Ueno Park beckons the pleasure-seeker for a stroll, a museum visit, or a concert. The stroller may wander among shrines and temples, or visit the zoo or aquarium. The museum-fancier will not miss the important National Museum with some 86000 exhibits memorializing Japan's history, art, and folklore, and will still have wide choice among the well-known Metropolitan Fine Art Gallery, the Museum of Western Art, the Gallery of Far Eastern Art and the National Science Museum. The concert-goer joins other music lovers at the Bunka Concert Hall, internationally praised for its fine acoustics.

Left The top of one of Tokyo's towering skyscrapers. These buildings are constructed to withstand even strong earthquakes.

South of the palace on a hill in Shiba Park, the Tokyo Tower thrusts 1098ft (333m) into the sky – 43ft (13m) higher than the Eiffel Tower on which it was patterned. Built in 1958, the Tower is a visible expression of Japan's recovery after World War II. The lucky among the four million annual visitors might catch sight of Mount Fuji along with the thrilling vista of the mammoth city. Significance as a landmark is matched by importance as a transmission center for seven television stations and numerous radio sets and systems. Sensitive instruments housed in the Tower measure Tokyo's pollution level and monitor vibrations in the earth.

Below The National Stadium. Built for the 1964 Olympics, it is a supreme example of modern Japanese architecture.

Facing, top A street fortune teller. Modern Japanese follow the old custom of consulting a fortune teller on all kinds of personal and business affairs. The seers, mostly astrologers and palmists, usually set up their booths around dusk along the main shopping thoroughfares.

Above A midtown movie house. Movies have a big and enthusiastic audience in Japan. Its own film industry is active and healthy, and foreign films are shown frequently. These are subtitled rather than dubbed, so tourists can generally find a film in their own language somewhere in the city.

Left Roller skating at the National Stadium in Yoyogi Park. Tokyo boasts of at least six huge sports complexes as well as smaller arenas and grounds.

Two of the country's most famous traditional gardens grace Tokyo. The Korakuen dates from 1626, the city's oldest, and the Rikugien from the 18th century. Both are entrancing havens from the hubbub of the city, within easy walks of subway or rail stations. Indeed, Tokyo provides a noteworthy network of public transportation, including 10 subway lines and a greater number of railroads. The bus service is first-rate, but confounds the users by lack of clear information. Most transportation is publicly owned and operated. That its excellence is marred by distressful overcrowding is no fault of the first rate system.

Right A viewing point on the lake in Happo-en Garden. The Happo-en Park is a small gem, exquisitely laid out in the traditional manner. It is so popular with wedding couples that their ceremonies become a kind of assembly line production, especially on astrologically good days.

Facing, top A clear view of the moat separating the main business district from the Imperial Palace. Now, as from the beginning, the palace is the center of the city.

Facing, bottom Tokyo's waterfront at night. It is a breathtaking sight when seen from one of the boats plying the Sumida River on the return trip from Asakusa.

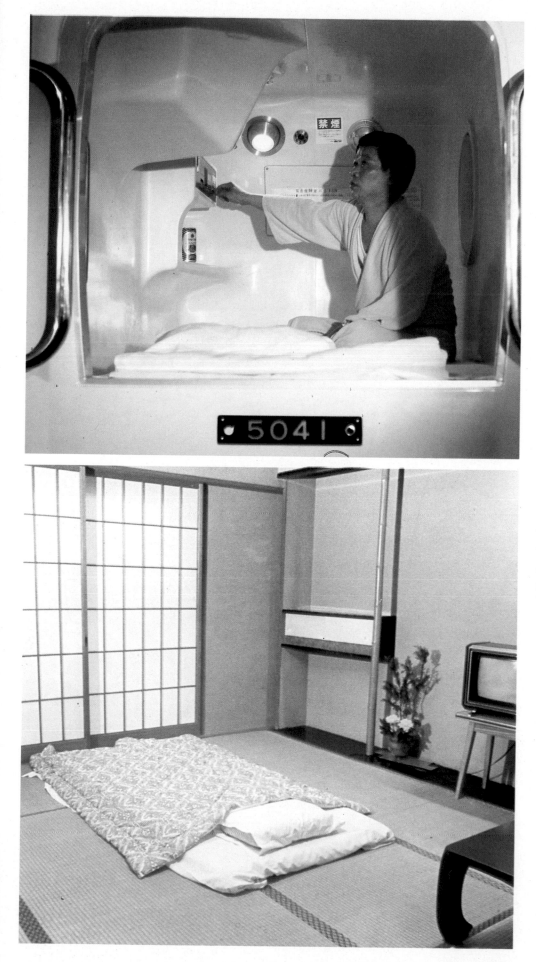

Facing, top left Shinjuku on an ordinary day. Trains rattle overhead, cars and trucks roar along the streets, and the crowds surge towards their various goals. In its earliest days, Shinjuku was a posting station – which perhaps explains why it grew into one of the city's busiest traffic junctions. Its shopping center east of the station is the second largest in Tokyo.

Facing, top right A ticket machine at a subway station. Always-in-a-hurry Tokyo dwellers save time by using the ticket dispensing machines at the entrances of subway and train stations. They are quick and efficient, returning change for overpayment and giving change for bills.

Facing, bottom The city at night with Mount Fuji in the distance. Once the people of Tokyo could see their beloved Fuji-san from any high point in the city. Now it's a rare day when the sky is unpolluted enough to reveal the majestic, mysterious mountain.

Above left A capsule hotel. Its tiny rooms of about the size of a pullman train berth have only bed, light, and radio and every room is the same. The nickname "capsule" certainly fits. Such hotels in major cities speak graphically of the chronic overcrowding – and of the accepting and adaptable nature of the Japanese people.

Left A room in a ryokan, or traditional inn. Soft tatami matting for the floor, white paper shoji screens at the windows, a futon for a bed, a tasteful flower arrangement and low lacquer tables – the simplicity and elegance are as Japanese in spirit as anything can be. However, today Tokyo has many more Western style hotels than ryokan, which do not offer modern conveniences – except for television.

The Working City

Commuter travel creates its own mythology. For example there's the story of the woman who stopped taking a packed lunch to work because it was always mashed to a pulp by the time she arrived. And the one about the man whose toggle buttons were ripped off his coat as a horde surged past at a station. The notorious rush-hour "pushers" actually exist. It is their job to stand outside the train doors and shove in already sardined passengers until not even a hairline space is visible between the long-suffering commuters.

Yes, monumental crowding is probably the most pervasive fact of daily life for Tokyo dwellers. They have tiny cramped homes, they are squeezed for space at work, they are part of a teeming mass at all entertainment and recreational facilities. In making the best of it, they have become so naturally sociable that they freely form close-knit groups of schoolmates, co-workers and neighbors. They usually take vacations, play sports and go on outings as a little crowd of their own. This adaption and a social etiquette based on formalized politeness make the temper of the gigantic city surprisingly benign.

The true Edoko (child of Edo) is rare, for only those who have lived in Tokyo — once Edo — for three generations qualify for the name. Older Edokos must be bewildered by the dizzying change in their hometown in the post-war period, but they probably do not bemoan it too much. The Japanese have always had a love for the new and different, with a long tradition of borrowing what they find interesting or progressive from other cultures. Their genius for putting their own stamp on things has kept such borrowing from being mere copying. So

Colorful carp streamers fly from poles on May 5 to announce that there is a boy living in the house nearby. It is to celebrate Children's Day, renamed from Boys' Day but observed in the old customary way. The carp symbolizes energy, ambition, and determination — qualities looked for in the son of the house. Children's Day is part of "golden week" when several national holidays in a row give everyone a week off.

the Edoko, along with the others, finds a place in everyday life for all sorts of modern electronics, takes all sorts of city face-lifting in stride, and happily anticipates the next innovation, fad, or gimmick.

Even though customs are changing, a woman's life is by and large still centered around the home, and wives might find themselves keeping dinner waiting for hours while their husbands are having a convivial time with office colleagues. It must be said that the social pressure on men to hobnob after work is great, especially when the boss suggests it, but the habit makes it hard for couples inclined

toward a more shared family life. Sunday is the big family day, when father for once is a part of whatever is going on. This might be an all-day excursion to the nearest large department store, which offers everything from roof garden play areas to art exhibitions, to hamburgers or raw fish meals. Or it might be to one of the city's parks such as the popular Shinjuku Gyoen, whose huge glasshouses of tropical and subtropical plants draw the crowds. This park is also a favorite of the city folk for the activity known as cherry blossom viewing, when people seek out and admire the trees in bloom – and sometimes picnic noisily

beneath their boughs. There is also a season and favored sites for plum blossom, chrysanthemum and iris viewing, which give even citified Japanese a way of expressing a deep love of nature.

Changing times have not altered the affection for and wide use of public baths by a people almost obsessed about personal cleanliness. They go to the local bath house, which stays open until midnight, for a clubby atmosphere in which to meet, talk and relax as well as to wash. Many go out of need, of course, because numerous homes still lack private baths. Yet it is a striking feature of Tokyo's millions

that hardly anyone is dirty, no matter how poor they are.

A custom that many modern Japanese wish they could forsake is that of formalized gift giving. The occasions calling for a gift are many, and the nature of the gift is bound by rigid convention: it has to be of exactly the right type and price. This is so vital and so problematical that people are brought to the verge of a nervous breakdown over the matter. The obligation also hits their budget rather hard.

Time off in tear-ahead Japan seldom means a personal vacation of any length, though in theory good paid vacations are

Below left The swimming pool at Korakuen Park. How can anyone swim its length or take a lap round? Real swimmers try to go early to beat the crowd. Paddlers and sunbathers simply find a tiny spot to claim as their own for a time.

Below An apartment building in the Tokyo suburbs. often a family of three or four will have a home of only one room in such a dwelling. The custom of sleeping on a futon, which can be easily folded for daytime storage, helps save space. The regular airing of this bedding on balcony rails is a common sight. It is also in keeping with the fastidious housekeeping of the people.

43

there to be taken. So the nine national holidays throughout the year give people a welcome break from the workaday routine. In one case, this break is like a countrywide vacation because most people take the whole of "golden week" off. This special week starts with the celebration of the emperor's birthday on April 29. May Day on the first is not an official holiday, but parades and events by the labor movement gather a multitude. Constitution Day is on May 3, and it's a new holiday commemorating the post-war constitution that went into effect in 1947. Then comes Children's Day on May 5, renamed from Boy's Day but observed like the old festival it was. Huge streamers in the color and shape of carp are flown from high poles, and boys everywhere set up a large tiered display unit to show off their collection of miniature drums, horses and male dolls costumed as of old.

Above left The Odakyu Department Store with its decorative night lighting. Whole families often spend Sunday at their local department store as the treat of the week. It is easy to find amusement there, what with children's play areas, rooftop cafés and many other kinds of eateries, special art and crafts exhibits, and classes in flower arranging or the tea ceremony among the usual offerings. A bit of shopping never goes amiss either.

Left The main entrance of the Mitsukoshi Department Store on the Ginza. The golden lion is a landmark of Tokyo, as is the store itself. The oldest department store in the city, the Mitsukoshi building survived the great earthquake of 1923. It is one of the quality shops, but shares a reputation for extraordinarily good service with all its competitors.

Facing A stall specializing in dried fish products. Numerous tiny shops are open to the elements and to all the passersby in every part of the city. Even though many people now shop in supermarkets, the old way of buying individual items from stall to stall is still holding its own.

The other long break consists of the first three days of January, when almost all businesses shut down. New Year's Day is the most important holiday of the year. It is customarily celebrated with a visit to the Meiji Shrine or the Kannon Temple, and many women and girls don their best kimono for the occasion. People eat omochi (rice cakes) and other special dishes, visit family, and exchange gifts. On January 2 the palace grounds are open to the public — which takes up the invitation in droves — and the emperor appears several times to wave greetings. Although New Year's Eve is not a national holiday, great numbers travel to be with relatives and see the New Year in at midnight by eating osoba (long buckwheat noodles) to symbolize a long and healthily austere life. The big bronze bells of Tokyo's major temples are tolled 108 times by teams of men wielding a thick log. This tradition occurs throughout Japan. The task is arduous but those chosen consider it an honor.

Right A typical bar in an old section of Tokyo. Sake, a rice wine about the strength of sherry which is drunk warm, is the national drink. Almost all bars close at midnight.

Below A dinner party in the traditional manner — all men sit cross-legged on cushions on the floor at low tables. One person always pours the sake for another — and the cup must never be empty.

Above left A street artist working with brush and ink. Many of these artists are so deft that they can complete a complicated drawing, such as this pair of writhing snakes, without lifting the brush from the paper. They usually finish to a round of applause from the admiring onlookers, who may also be potential customers.

Above Tokyo teenagers with the black leather look. They appear to be sinister, but violent crime is an almost unknown problem in this huge metropolis.

Left A sidewalk shoeshiner at work. Shoeshiners, many of them women, offer their fast adroit service on the street outside some of the main railroad stations, especially Ueno. In fact, shoemakers who mend heels and soles are also found there, doing a speedy and cheap repair job.

Today it is no longer essential for the well-bred young woman to be skilled in ikebana (flower arranging) and the tea ceremony, although both pursuits are still popular. Young men are likely to be fanatical about baseball while still having a favorite sumo wrestler. And company tycoons may be bitten by the golf bug while still practicing the art of calligraphy. Contemporary Tokyo looks like many a Western city, but the flavor of life is still essentially Japanese.

Below Celebrating the New Year. New Year is the most important holiday of the year and a day for a big feast. As usual, the food is artistically arranged and served on dishes of a size and shape to set it off to best advantage. Most families have special lacquerware and other tableware kept for use only on this holiday.

Below The Kanda festival. Every other year in mid May the pageantry of the festival connected with the local Myojin Shrine fills the streets of Kanda district. Part of the ceremonial event is the bearing of a portable shrine in procession, and it takes 16 men to carry the palanquin on which this object of respect rests. The Japanese people love their festivals, which are an important part of national culture. Many of these fall in the spring and autumn and have associations with nature. The Kanda festival, like a number of others throughout the year, is very much a neighborhood affair. Those chosen for the hard task of shouldering the palanquin consider it an honor.

5
Living Traditions

Japanese culture is rich with art forms but even everyday things are imbued with beauty. The humblest corner shop will produce a little work of art in wrapping an ordinary purchase. And the most modest eatery will present food to delight the eyes as much as the stomach. Taste and style seem to permeate everything so that even the most common household item reflects the care that has been taken in matching the material to the design. This sense of the beautiful seems innate but has been handed down from one generation to the next and been sharpened by a long and rich artistic heritage.

A night at Tokyo's Kabukiza Theater: here is traditional theater of a spectacular kind. Kabuki originated in the 17th century as popular dramatic entertainment, opposed to aristocratic court entertainment. It is drama, mime, dance, and music all in one. It can intoxicate the senses with its gorgeous costumes, striking make-up, and dazzling stage effects. In fact, Kabuki audiences of some 300 years ago were the first in the world to be spellbound by the wonders of the revolving stage, a Japanese theatrical invention of major importance. Often the

Previous page Geisha, with their gorgeous and expensive kimono, whitened faces, and elaborate hairdos, are immediately recognized as nothing but Japanese. Their role too is very much a part of Japanese culture: they provide company and entertainment for men whose lifestyle seldom finds them at home while women rarely go out. Geisha are trained from an early age to sing, dance, play musical instruments and converse wittily.

Below A sumō match. In a land of generally small and wiry people, the giant wrestlers of enormous weight are a startling sight. However, their limberness and sometimes grace in the preliminary rituals of the match are remarkable. The most famous of them are national heroes. There are three two-week tournaments a year in Tokyo in May, September, and January. Tickets are hard to get, so television audiences are large.

favorite actors are the onnagata, men who by tradition play the female roles—and without a trace of transvestite titillation. Modern audiences seldom understand the old stylized language of the plays, but true fans are so familiar with the plots that they can follow every shade of meaning and feeling. They are helped by the unique style of acting in which certain supercharged poses accentuate dramatic points. A Kabuki performance lasts for hours and offers a spectacle unlike any other.

The classical Noh drama was the court theater of the 14th century and contrasts with Kabuki in every way except the splendor of some of the costumes. The stage setting is always the same and always static: bare but for a back panel decorated with a single twisted pine tree. There is almost no action in the plots and the movements of the performers are mannered, studied, and slowed almost to a standstill. Masks tell the audience who the characters are supposed to be, and these masks are often valued heirlooms of the past. There are some devotees of Noh theater, but not enough to support it. However the government subsidizes this art form because of its historical and cultural importance.

Bunraku is puppet theater of a fascinating complexity. The youngest of the three forms of classical entertainment, it was invented in the mid-18th century. Three skilled manipulators dressed all in black are in full view as they make the 3ft (1m) high puppets move their head, eyes and mouth, arms and legs, and even fingers. Professional storytellers sit at the side of the stage and recite the plays in the old manner, accompanied by musicians playing the samisen, a stringed instrument somewhat like a banjo. The puppets wear costumes nearly as sumptuous as those of Kabuki, and the intricate manipulation makes them appear surprisingly human. This three-in-one amalgam of puppetry, recitation and music was created in Osaka, and the national company regularly tours from there to Tokyo to perform.

Tokyo's museums and galleries entice art lovers with their galaxy of traditional paintings. From the first, Japanese painters worked with watercolors and sumi ink on thin paper or silk. Their work was in the form of single hanging scrolls or long rolled scrolls. By the end of the 12th century the yamato-e, or native, style of painting had been established: long scrolls of rich color, dreamy treatment, and related scenes

Left and below Scenes from two kabuki plays: kabuki is one of the classical theater forms, renowned for sumptuous costumes, spectacular stage effects, and romantic stories. It dates from the seventeenth century and was the popular drama of the day, as opposed to the theater of the nobility. The actors always play the same types, such as hero or villain, and come from the same family in a long line of performers. Traditionally men play the female roles and these actors, called onnagata (females) have always been among the most popular. Women have recently taken roles, but only outside the country. Performances, which last for long hours, take place in the Kabukiza Theater in the Ginza district. The building looks like a shrine — and indeed is a shrine to the fervid fans of this exciting blend of drama, music, dance ,and mime all in one.

following one after another like a "moving picture". From the 14th century onwards landscape became the most important subject, and the most influential school of painting produced masterpieces characterized by bold brush strokes, concentrated simplicity, and an off-center focus in which unfilled space was an important part of the composition. One of the thriving art forms of the late 16th to the mid-17th centuries was the panelled screen.

The most famous examples of this were painted in thick strong colors on a splendid goldleaf background. Birds, flowers and animals were always favored as subjects by the nature-loving Japanese artists.

During the 18th and 19th centuries there was a mass market for the woodblock prints known as ukiyo-e (floating world paintings). These were mostly story illustrations, vivid scenes of everyday city life – including lowlife – and brilliant

portraits of popular entertainers. They were scorned by the art world of their day, but ukiyo-e are now what most of the world thinks of and admires as Japanese art.

Happily it is not necessary to go to a museum to enjoy or buy traditional pottery, lacquerware and other handicrafts. Shops and department stores abound with them, both old and new. Of course, a trip to the Japan Folkcraft Museum in suburban Tokyo will reveal the best of the ages, but even

Above A Ko-Kutani pitcher of the late eighteenth to early nineteenth century. This type of overglaze decorated porcelain came mainly from Kaga. In contrast to such highly patterned porcelain, Japanese stoneware is simple in the extreme. The most prized is often squat and irregular in shape, subtle and earthy in color, informal and practical.

Right A woodblock print by Kitagawa Utamaro showing a night out in the amusement quarters of old. Such prints, bold and lively, were often illustrations for stories that had a mass market in seventeenth and eighteenth century Tokyo. Today they are admired worldwide as some of the finest output of Japanese artists, but in their own day they were considered vulgar and inferior.

Left A cherry blossom viewing-party in Ueno Park. Even though the pace of life is hectic, the city people take time to show their love of nature by going to look at the blossoming cherry trees in April. Sometimes the parties beneath the boughs get boisterous, but the point of the visit is to think upon the beautiful fragility of life, symbolized by the short-lived flowers. Later in the spring come plum blossom and iris, and chrysanthemums take the limelight in autumn. All the city parks are crammed on these occasions, but certain favorite ones for each particular flower become almost impenetrable.

Below Springtime blossom viewing at the Meiji Shrine. The inner gardens of the shrine is where everyone wants to be in May when more than a hundred varieties of iris are at their best.

most of the modern mass-produced work is worthy. All Japanese craftwork has a distinctive regional character because of the old custom by which leading artisans stayed and worked in their local communities, passing on their techniques from generation to generation. There are still hundreds of small pottery centers in the country, each known for their own special glazes, colors, and designs, and much of the present-day factory-made pottery keeps the regional touches. Stoneware ceramics owe their great popularity to the unique tea ceremony that flourished from

Facing The Zojoji Temple. Set in lovely Shiba Park, this temple was built in 1605 and is a fine example of traditional architecture. It was badly damaged both in the earthquake of 1923 and the bombing of 1945, and the Main Hall was reconstructed in faithful detail in 1974.

Right The heron dance, performed as part of the Asakusa spring festival on 8 April. This festival is small in scale and is celebrated in only two places in the country – here and a district of Kyoto. The heron is a good luck symbol in Japan.

Below A sidewalk peddler in an old part of the city. His meager wares tell the story of his low economic status.

Below How sushi is served. The arrangement of each piece of food in relation to the other, and on the natural wood slab that sets off color, is an example of the everyday art of creating visual appeal.

the 16th century on. Part of the ritual was to appreciate the beauty of the tea-bowls, and the stamp of beauty came to be rugged shape and subdued coloring. In one kind of prized pottery the surface was always left natural to receive any markings that came by chance in the firing.

The production of lacquerware probably dates from 3000 years ago, but the use of gold and silver dust in lacquering was brought to a high art form during the 14th and 15th centuries. This most luxurious kind of lacquerware was meant for the aristocracy, but even ordinary people had other kinds for grand occasions such as New Year's and weddings. The most notable period for lacquerware was in the late 16th and early 17th centuries when the

foremost practitioners made the pampas grass, chrysanthemum, bush clover and wild pink everlasting favorites for decoration. Today's lacquerware is not hand-crafted by artisans with a touch of genius, but factory-made. However the manufactured product is still of a fine quality and retains the elegance and imagination of its forerunners.

Bottom A menu display of plastic food in the window of a restaurant. This unique way of showing what is on offer is most helpful, as well as being a kind of commercial art form. The plastic replicas look real enough to eat. They are used by all but the most expensive restaurants or those specializing in only one dish.

Below A street vendor in a northwest suburb. The delectable offering is okonomiyaki, a pancake with various fillings. It makes a quick cheap meal and, because of the care taken by most Japanese cooks, will probably taste as good as it looks.

6
Getting Away

Even the greatest of cities can sometimes pall, both for those who live in them and those who are visiting. Tokyo dwellers are fortunate in their choice of interesting and accessible spots for a day trip or weekend jaunt, and they take advantage of their opportunities with enthusiasm. Where do they go? Among the favorites are Mount Fuji, Hakone, Kamakura, and Nikko.

Mount Fuji

The snow-clad volcano that the people affectionately call Fuji-san, a perfect cone in shape, is one of the most famous mountains in the world. The Japanese are fond of saying that their beloved Fuji-san never looks the same twice, and generations of travel writers have confirmed that the swirling clouds and changing light alter its appearance constantly. Mount Fuji last sprinkled Tokyo streets with ash in December 1707. It has an emotional hold on the people and has inspired innumerable Japanese artists and poets to try to express its mysterious beauty with brushstrokes and words. In fact, the painter Hokusai earned his reputation in the West with his *Views of*

Mount Fuji, affectionately known as Fuji-san in the form of address used for people, is one of the most instantly recognizable landmarks in the world. Generations of artists and writers, especially poets, have tried to express its bewitching beauty and its almost mythical attraction.

Below Fuji-san as seen from Lake Ashi in Hakone. The boat ride around the lake gives visitors the chance to view snowclad Mount Fuji from many angles. The perfectly cone-shaped mountain has a mysterious emotional hold on the Japanese — and travelers who watch it change constantly in swirling mists begin to understand their fascination.

Mount Fuji painted in the 19th century. This series of pictures are among the best known in all of art history.

There was a time when this volcano was considered sacred. People worshipped it and climbers made the laborious ascent to 12 390 ft (3776 m) as pilgrims. Now about 100 000 Japanese climb to the summit yearly, following six well-worn paths in a steady stream that marks the way for everyone. The ascent takes nine hours and can only be undertaken from the beginning of July to the end of August because of snow in the other months. Of the throngs that visit Mount Fuji without necessarily making the climb – more than 300 000 a year – many take one-day excursions to the base. For weekend and longer stays, the Five Lakes region at the northern base serves Tokyo as part of a huge new recreational area.

Once the people of Tokyo could see and marvel at Mount Fuji, 44 miles (71 km) away, from most high points in the city. Now, except on rare occasions, the mountain is obscured by heavy air pollution. However, this does not seem to diminish the hold that it has on the Japanese people.

Hakone

Day visitors to Hakone from Tokyo are counted not in the thousands but in the millions, especially at weekends. They swarm into this old resort 62 miles (100 km) away on the shores of Lake Ashi to view Mount Fuji from its southern aspect. Those who happen to get a clear, calm day rejoice in their luck, for they will see the reflection of Fuji-san in the lake's waters. It is this sight that has made Hakone famous and long-lived, though the local shrine and graceful red torii (gate) near the lakeside have many admirers too.

The area around Hakone is dotted with hot springs, which are a favorite retreat for the big city dwellers. A good soak in sulfurous hot waters seems to have magical powers of rejuvenation. Visitors certainly leave refreshed and invigorated if not literally younger!

Left Hakone's lakeshore. This old resort, ever popular for its good view of Fuji-san, attracts millions of day visitors from Tokyo at the weekends. The nearby hot springs are another draw, as is the charm of the small town itself.

Above left The Hakone open air museum which contains Japanese and Western sculpture in a garden setting. It is a more recent addition to the resort's tourist offerings.

Above Detail of one of the dazzling gates in Nikko, home of the Toshogu Shrines of the Tokugawa shoguns. All of Nikko is a glow of gold leaf and red lacquer on buildings of unsurpassed magnificence. The splendor is almost dreamlike, and will linger in the mind for a long time.

Right Part of Nikko's picturesque Thousand Person Procession. Every May a thousand men, women, and children don the often brilliant attire of the seventeenth and eighteenth centuries and march through the town. It is an exciting and eye-filling event that recreates the days of the shoguns, to whom Nikko owes all its overwhelming splendor.

Kamakura

For 141 years, between the late 12th and early 14th centuries, the seaside city of Kamakura was the nerve center of the nation, and that epoch became known as the Kamakura Period. Kamakura is no longer so important but enjoys great popularity as a resort, particularly during the summer months when its sandy beaches are crammed with Tokyo vacationers.

The focus of a visit to Kamakura, only a half hour from Tokyo by train, is the Daibutsu (Great Buddha). This 40 ft (13 m) high, 100-ton bronze statue has to be one of the world's most-photographed objects. It emanates an aura of calm and is universally praised for its beauty. The Daibutsu has stood in the Kotokuin temple since 1252, a tribute to the art and technology of the past and a constant source of pleasure.

In the city that introduced Buddhism into Japan, it is natural that the principal sights are temples and shrines. Some 80 of them nestle in secluded corners, and their contents include many objects classed as an Important Cultural Property or a National Treasure. Visitors with a special interest in temple architecture and artifacts will be captivated by Kamakura but the less enthusiastic will find reward enough in two or three of the best-known temples. One of these is the Engakuji, the country's oldest establishment of the Zen sect. It was built in 1282 and its bronze temple bell, cast in 1301, is designated a National Treasure.

The Gokurakuji, dating from 1259, is especially rich in classified art treasures in the form of stone and wooden statues and bronze bells. The Hase Kannon contains a famous 11-headed Goddess of Mercy statue. Sculpted from a single tree trunk, the 27 ft (8 m) high Kannon is the tallest wooden image in Japan. The Zuisenji temple is noted for its beautiful Zen garden rich with plum blossoms, and the Tokeyi temple is famed for having been founded as a sanctuary for maltreated women.

Nikko

Splendor . . . grandeur . . . bedazzlement. These are the kind of words that can be applied to Nikko, the little hill town made gorgeous and famous by the shrine of the first Tokugawa shogun. This Toshogu shrine is truly a sight to behold with its magnificent buildings of red lacquer and metal leaf,

Left A thrilling vista from Nikko's nearby hills. The National Park in the environs of Nikko boasts the highest waterfall in the country, and the route along 48 cliffhanging hairpin curves provides a special kind of adventure.

65

much decorated and embellished. Here is the impressive five-story pagoda, one of whose panels is intricately carved with the three monkeys depicting see no evil, speak no evil, and hear no evil. And here's the Yomeimon (Gate of Sunlight), so lavishly decorated that people have been known to gaze at it for hours. Here is the sacred red bridge, trodden by no one except the shogun and the emperor's emissaries for 200 years. Here in May is the picturesque and exciting Thousand Person Procession, in which that number parade in the shogunate costumes of the 17th and 18th centuries.

Add natural scenic beauty to the artistic achievement of Nikko and it is clear why its 93-mile (150-km) distance from Tokyo is so well-traveled. Near Nikko in the inviting National Park of hills, lakes, and rivers, is the highest waterfall in the country. It is a breathtaking spectacle, but one of the roads which leads to it is breathtaking in a different way, having no less than 48 harrowing hairpin turns to it.

Below The stunning Yomeimon, or Gate of Sunlight, of the Toshogu Shrine. It has so much ornamentation to look at that people often gaze at it for hours on end.

Right The Sankei-en Garden in Yokohama. This delightful large garden is one of Yokohama's only beauty spots. The busy seaport near Tokyo is mostly of interest as the first big foreign settlement after the nineteenth-century opening of Japan to trade.

Below The Daibutsu, or Great Buddha, of Kamakura. Countless visitors have marveled at the serene beauty of this huge bronze statue dating from 1252. In fact, it is one of the world's most photographed objects.

Major Attractions

1 Asakusa Kannon Temple. Also known as the Sensoji Temple, it is named after the Kannon or Goddess of Mercy to whom the tall main hall is dedicated. Said to have been founded in the seventh century by three fishermen, who found in their nets one day a tiny image of Kannon only 2 in (5 cm) in height.

2 Kabukiza Theater. Here the traditional Japanese theater with marvelous costumes and highly stylized acting is performed. Kabuki plays are performed almost year-round in at least one of the kabuki theaters in Tokyo.

3 Ginza. The nation's most famous shopping district, with long established and prestigious department stores and shopping buildings. It's a district filled with sidestreets and fringed by large and small specialty shops, restaurants and coffee shops, bars and night clubs, mostly exclusive and expensive.

4 Meiji Shrine. The shrine stands in an extensive thickly-wooded parkland, and is dedicated to the Emperor Meiji and his Consort. It's a particularly fine example of Shinto architecture.

5 Roppongi. This is an entertainment district with a lively and sophisticated atmosphere. With masses of coffee shops, bars, pubs and restaurants – mostly in the inexpensive to moderate price range – it's a good place to visit, and if you like dancing then you'll find a whole host of fashionable discotheques.

6 Tokyo National Museum. This is the largest museum in Japan with over 86,000 objects associated with Japanese and Far Eastern ancient and medieval art. Also within the vicinity of Ueno Park.

7 Akihabara. This is the district where one electronics shop after another offer myriads of products from which the tourist can choose. A must for anyone in search of the latest electronic gadgetry.

8 Imperial Palace. Within the Imperial Palace grounds it is possible to find remains of the former Edo Castle, some imposing gateways and guard towers, Nijubashi Bridge, Imperial Palace Plaza and the East Garden. The Emperor's Palace lies beyond the thickly wooded stone-walled palace grounds.

9 Koraku.

10 Rikugien Park. One of Tokyo's finest examples of a typical Japanese landscape garden. It was originally laid out in the 18th century and was a favorite garden of Tsunayoshi, the fifth Tokugawa Shogun.

11 Tokyo Tower. Is a 1092 ft (333 m) high independent steel tower and is both a telecasting and an entertainment center, housing various exhibition halls, shops and restaurants. A superb view of the entire city of Tokyo and Tokyo Bay can be obtained from the observation platforms.

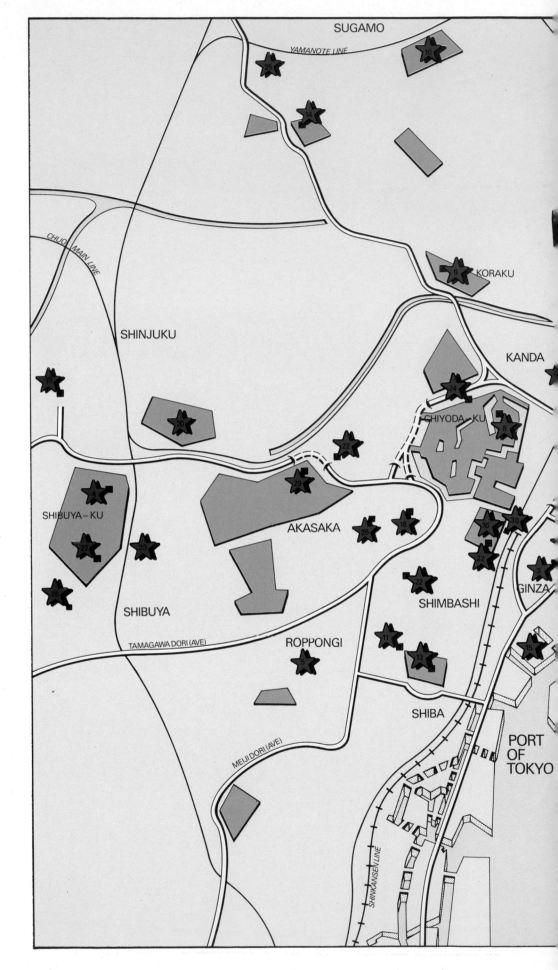

12 Ueno Park and vicinity. This is a stroll into history and culture amid unsurpassed natural scenery. Within the vicinity of the park you'll find the Ueno Zoo, Toshogu Shrine, the Shinobazu Pond and the National Science Museum.

13 Zojoji Temple. Formerly the family temple of the Tokugawas, it contains many cultural objects. The red-lacquered two-story Main Gate, built in 1605, is included among the nation's "Important Cultural Properties".

14 Gokukuji Temple.

15 Hama Detached Palace Gardens.

16 Hibiya Park. This park is situated in front of the Imperial Hotel, with Kasumigaseki's office buildings at its back. This park is a favorite relaxing place for Tokyo office workers. There are occasional lunchtime concerts in the summer.

17 Kanda. If you're in the mood for a book browse then visit Kanda. Here one street is lined with more than a hundred second-hand bookshops, helping to make this district one of the largest concentrations of booksellers in the world.

18 National Diet Building. Stands overlooking the Kasumigaseki district of the city. It's an imposing tower which presides over Japan's administrative center. Government, ministry and agency buildings cluster in this area.

19 Shinjuku Skyscrapers. Within Skyscraper Street there are a series of ultra-modern high-rise buildings. Some are modern hotels, and others are office buildings on the upper floors of which are a number of restaurants. Of course the views are excellent.

20 Shinjuku Gyoen National Garden. Formerly the property of the Imperial family, this is now one of Tokyo's largest and most popular parks for strolling and admiring the flowering shrubs and foliage. Highlights are the cherry blossoms in April and the chrysanthemums in early November.

21 Nihonbashi. This is the bridge at the top of Ginza and is the point from which all distances are measured. It has been rebuilt several times.

22 Imperial Hotel, Hotel Okura, New Otani Hotel.

23 Harajuku. In the fashionable part of Tokyo, Harajuku's symbol is Omote-sando, a wide boulevard fringed by restaurants, attractive coffee shops, small boutiques and interesting specialty shops. Omote-sando leads up to the Meiji Shrine.

24 National Museum of Modern Art. A four-story building displaying paintings, woodblock prints, sculptures and other objects of art produced in the 20th century.

25 Sunshine City. The "City" is dominated by the 60-story Sunshine 60 building, the tallest in Asia. The fastest elevator in the world whisks you to the sixtieth floor observatory in only 35 seconds. An aquarium, theater and the Orient Museum are also in the Sunshine City's compound.

26 Japan Folkcrafts Museum. You'll find traditional folkcrafts collected by Soetsu Yanagi, housed in his former home. The very best of all ages is to be found here.

27 Yoyogi Park. This is the former site of the Tokyo Olympic Village and is a quiet thickly-wooded park with a wild bird sanctuary, a children's playground and a cycling course.

28 Akasaka. This is a traditional geisha district, and you're likely to see rickshaws carrying their gorgeously-dressed passengers through the sidestreets in the early evening. Akasaka is also home for some of Tokyo's most exclusive and expensive nightclubs.

29 Akasaka Detached Palace. The Palace is almost an extension of the Imperial Palace. It was built in 1909 for the Crown Prince, and, since 1974, has been used as a state guest house.

30 Marunouchi. Lies between Tokyo Station and the Imperial Palace, and is Tokyo's business center. Tall buildings standing side by side contain the headquarters of the leading banks and trading firms.

PICTURE CREDITS